John Gardner: A Tiny Eulogy

John Gardner

A Tiny Eulogy

Phil Jourdan

dead letter office

BABEL Working Group

punctum books ✶ brooklyn, ny

JOHN GARDNER: A TINY EULOGY
© Phil Jourdan, 2012.

This work is licensed under the Creative Commons Attribution-NonCommercial-NoDerivs 3.0 Unported License. To view a copy of this license, visit: http://creativecommons.org/licenses/by-nc-nd/3.0, or send a letter to Creative Commons, 444 Castro Street, Suite 900, Mountain View, California, 94041, USA.

This work is Open Access, which means that you are free to copy, distribute, display, and perform the work as long as you clearly attribute the work to the authors, that you do not use this work for commercial gain in any form whatsoever, and that you in no way alter, transform, or build upon the work outside of its normal use in academic scholarship without express permission of the author and the publisher of this volume. For any reuse or distribution, you must make clear to others the license terms of this work.

First published in 2012 by
Dead Letter Office, BABEL Working Group
an imprint of punctum books
Brooklyn, New York
http://punctumbooks.com

The BABEL Working Group is a collective and desiring-assemblage of scholar-gypsies with no leaders or followers, no top and no bottom, and only a middle. BABEL roams and stalks the ruins of the post-historical university as a multiplicity, a pack, looking for other roaming packs and multiplicities with which to cohabit and build temporary shelters for intellectual vagabonds. We also take in strays.

ISBN-10: 0615734510
ISBN-13: 978-0615734514

Cover image adapted from Peter Dranitsin, *Follow Me to Heaven* (2009).

Table of Contents

Introduction	1
Gardner, Art, and Philosophy	7
Theorizing the Good	13
Theorizing the True	19
Is Moral Fiction the Fiction of Moralists?	26
Moral Fiction and Plot	31
Writers of Fiction and Writers of Criticism	34
Goodnight, Gardner	42
References	45

For Michael Hulse, who has been a friend, a hero, and a most excellent dude for help with my writing

John Gardner: A Tiny Eulogy

Phil Jourdan

> *What happens with writers is if you say something bad about them, and it seems wise and fair, their feelings are hurt, but they're not mad at you because writers are too serious to be mad at you when you tell the truth.*
>
> ~ John Gardner[1]

INTRODUCTION

A text as baffling as John Gardner's polemical manifesto, *On Moral Fiction* (1978), demands attention and forbids indifference. Gardner died young — but he lived long enough to see his career demolished after the publication of

---

[1] John Gardner, "Interview with John Gardner, English Department of Pan American University (1981)," in *Conversations with John Gardner*, ed. Allan Chavkin (Jackson: University Press of Mississippi, 1990), 259.

that hugely unpopular book. He was vilified, attacked from all angles (in literary journals as well as on television channels like PBS),[2] dismissed as a reactionary, and cut off from the literary circles he had once frequented. "I have not developed any enemies that I know of,"[3] he told an interviewer a year before the motorcycle accident that killed him. Yet whether or not he made any enemies, his book was appropriated by unwanted new friends: because of what was considered his highly conservative view of art, Gardner was approached by evangelists like Jerry Falwell as well as the American Nazi Party.[4] To this day he continues to be treated as a hysterical moralist even by otherwise careful critics like Wayne C. Booth. The pity of all of this is that, for its many flaws, *On Moral Fiction* is a book that deserves to be read, to be taken seriously, even to be read morally, as Gardner would have put it. My aim, then, is to accept, however briefly, this neglected challenge, and to take Gardner as he wanted to be taken. If he is doomed to literary oblivion, he has at least earned a proper funeral, attended by one or two friends who tried to understand.

The relationship between morality and art, of course, has been debated in various ways

---

[2] Barry Silesky, *John Gardner: Literary Outlaw* (Chapel Hill: Algonquin, 2004), 254.
[3] Gardner, "Interview with the English Department of Pan American University," 259.
[4] Silesky, *John Gardner: Literary Outlaw*, 256.

across the centuries, and Gardner's contribution to the conversation is decidedly old-fashioned. It is also resolutely difficult to make much sense out of this contribution. Doubtless, Gardner is passionate in his insistence that there is an ineradicable link between well-crafted fiction and a kind of heightened moral awareness. The problem, as I see it, is that by trying to be polemical instead of quietly effective, Gardner puts off potential allies and categorically misreads certain other novelists to make a point. He rejects almost all the fiction of his own time (he was working on this text in the mid-to-late 1970s) as somehow too clever or nihilistic or immoral, whatever that term has come to mean by the end of his book.

But suppose there is in fact an important message to be conveyed: that the most enduring works of fiction, those that "mean something" to readers of many generations, are those whose construction entails a kind of moral courage — what then? If most modern fiction is lacking in the way Gardner describes, then what can be done about it? The answer must partly be sought in Gardner's manifesto itself. It must also come from outside, from a careful preliminary formalization of the argument he puts forth that would resolve inconsistencies or remove them, and ignore the petty name-calling that constitutes whole chunks of the book.

To formalize, or theorize, John Gardner may

be to go against his wishes. Gardner is not a theorist. *On Moral Fiction* makes clear Gardner's distaste for grand theories that cannibalize other texts for self-confirmation. No room, in Gardner's view, for critics whose objectives lie in the explanation of literary pyrotechnics. "In all the arts, our criticism is for the most part inhumane," he claims. "We are rich in schools which speak of how art 'works' and avoid the whole subject of what work it ought to do."[5] The work it ought to do, as Gardner conceives it, is not always clearly explained. "The traditional view is that true art is moral: it seeks to improve life, not debase it. It seeks to hold off, at least for a while, the twilight of the gods and us" (5). These are grandiose words, and it cannot be doubted, on the evidence to be found in the pages of his manifesto, that Gardner is anything but serious. After all, art is "essentially serious and beneficial, a game played against chaos and death, against entropy" (6). Gardner is never totally precise in his formulation of what moral art should be, but we know that it "asserts and reasserts those values which hold off dissolution, struggling to keep the mind intact and preserve the city, the mind's safe preserve." And lastly: "Art rediscovers, generation by generation, what is necessary to

---

[5] John Gardner, *On Moral Fiction* (New York: Basic Books, 2000), 16 (hereafter cited parenthetically in my text, by page number).

humanness" (6).

What we are left with, by the time the first and most conventionally theoretical section of *On Moral Fiction* is over, is a collection of aphoristic glances into the eyes of the One True God of Moral Fiction. This is not merely ironic mockery — for it is never quite clear whether Gardner is hiding, in one of his pockets, a secret affinity to God and all that the word entails. Certainly "God" is a character in this book. So is "Truth." And those other obvious secondary characters, "Beauty" and "Goodness," also make their appearances. As for the protagonist, we have two possibilities. Either the hero of Gardner's tale is "Art," making "Morality" a mere sidekick — or it is the other way around. It is not always easy to tell where the stress falls. Sometimes Gardner seems simply to equate "good art" with "moral art." Sometimes, however, art as a whole is more like the father of a family of various troublesome or virtuous offspring: the black sheep of cynical postmodernism (Thomas Pynchon), the clumsy but deeply sincere eldest son (William Faulkner), the smart aleck or braggart (William Gass). In this scenario, Father Art is waiting for the prodigal child he has called Moral Fiction, the missing piece of the puzzle that would set the literary world right once and for all. Moral fiction is adventurous, not always obedient, and sometimes disappears from sight. But it is moral fiction that Gardner believes we need.

The purpose of my little "eulogy" is not to do John Gardner a favor and redeem his name. The impetus behind this is a conviction that the criticisms we can aim at Gardner (as a man, critic, novelist, thinker) are all too often diversionary. Nobody needs to approve of his methods or his bullying, or indeed to pay any attention to him as an intellectual at all, so long as his message is taken into account. And his message is a familiar but seemingly unpopular one: "What fiction does at its very best is test out values. . . . A good book leads to a great affirmation."[6] The belief that novels matter, not only as works of art, but also as experiments in which basic values to which we cling can be tested in safety, may seem unfashionable today, but it is a belief full of potential.

---

[6] Silesky, *John Gardner: Literary Outlaw*, 254.

Gardner, Art and Philosophy

Whatever moral fiction is, it is clearly not just another way of giving beauty and goodness the same ontological status. At no point does Gardner appear to claim that what is beautiful is by necessity also moral. In fact the purely aesthetic side of art, which according to a commonsense view might be the most important aspect, is sometimes conspicuously missing from Gardner's argument. He does write of the Beautiful, and we will look later at his treatment of this concept; but for the most part, "Gardnerian" moral fiction prizes something other than beauty-as-such.

"Art probes," Gardner tells us. "It stalks like a hunter lost in the woods, listening to itself and to everything around it, unsure of itself, waiting to pounce" (9). This probing is key. Serious art, Gardner seems to imply, is trying to find its way in the darkness into which we as a collective have allowed ourselves to slip. "Art is as original and important as it is precisely because it does not start out with a clear knowledge of what it means to say" (13). There is more: "Art, in sworn opposition to chaos, discovers by its process what it can say. That is art's morality. Its full meaning is beyond paraphrase" (14). One understands, then, that the process is part of the truth of moral art.

When Hegel, in the Preface to his *Phenomenology*, warns against seeing the truth of philosophy as somehow separable from the processes that lead us to it, he is arguing much the same thing, if we substitute "moral art" for "philosophy": "Whatever might be appropriately said about philosophy — say, a historical statement of the main drift and the point of view, the general content and results, a string of random assert-ions and assurances about truth — none of this can be accepted as the way in which to expound philosophical truth."[7] For all of his criticisms of philosophy's methods, Gardner is a Hegelian in this aspect. "Art," let us recall, "discovers by its process what it can say," and, indeed, its full meaning is "beyond paraphrase" (14).

Gardner, however, is unkind to the modern philosopher. "Philosophy is more concerned with coherence than with what William James called life's 'buzzing, blooming confusion'" (9). And: "Structuralists, formalists, linguistic philosophers who tell us that works of art are like trees — simply objects for perception — all avoid on principle the humanistic questions: who will this work of art help?" Unfortunately, "The business of criticism has become definition, morality reduced to the positivist

---

[7] Georg W. F. Hegel, *The Phenomenology of Spirit*, trans. Arthur V. Miller (Oxford: Oxford University Press, 1977), 1.

ideal of clarity" (17). If fiction needs to be made moral, so does criticism. The two go hand-in-hand. In fact, "like theology and religion," art and criticism "are basically companions but not always friends. At times they may be enemies" (8). They cannot be separated, but they needn't always get along.

Thus it would seem that Gardner wishes to do different things in *On Moral Fiction*. He wants to set a course for fiction writers here; but over there, he has in mind the task of the critic. On one page his goal is nothing less than to slash and burn everything he finds reprehensible. The next page he is less belligerent. His arguments are confused and at time confusing. One suspects, when reading his book for the first time, that Gardner is setting standards he wouldn't be able to reach in his own work; yet those standards are never explicitly formulated. They are not theorized. This is in keeping with his style, his beliefs and the message of his tract, but it is also a good way to leave a reader frustrated. Perhaps theorizing is totally beside the point — it would, in any case, radically transform Gardner's message, as one of his subtlest insights concerns the dynamism of the written word. To theorize would be to run the risk of being over-schematic already; in a sense it would be moralistic, a way of universalizing a set of rules for writing fiction that could help us to live morally.

The paradox is that Gardner seems both for and against this universality. On the one hand the values he champions would stand the test of time: true works of art "exert their civilizing influence century after century, long after the cultures that produced them have decayed" (105). This implies a set of standards to which "humanity" might adhere over the millennia. The fate of Achilles or the Karamazovs is, in this view, an eternally relatable fate. Dostoevsky's Russia is no more, and Homer lived centuries before Aristotle first laid out his own important rules for poetry and drama; and yet, for someone like Gardner, their works have endured because they were moral, because these authors were grappling with eternal truths.

On the other hand, Gardner is not so bold as to write out exactly what an eternal truth might be, what the substance of an enduring work might look like. A universal work might very well follow immutable laws, but these laws are not mere givens. They must be worked towards, on the assumption that with enough intellectual integrity and moral curiosity, their invisible presence will guide the work to its moral beauty. We are back to philosophy; "at its best fiction is . . . a way of thinking, a philosophical method" (107).

Probing and poking at cultural, intellectual and moral values is part of being an artist. Gardner evidently cherishes this aspect of the human inclination to art. Although there is an understandable prejudice among academics against writing books like *On Moral Fiction* because of their perceived anti-intellectualism, the fact is that Gardner never discourages intellectual or philosophical streaks in novels just for the sake of it. Undoubtedly a careless reading of *On Moral Fiction* could leave someone convinced that Gardner dislikes Saul Bellow and Thomas Pynchon because of their erudition. But that would, indeed, be a careless reading. Ideas are important for Gardner, but they must be used in specific ways. "A really good book tests ideas,"[8] as he says, and the goal of *On Moral Fiction* appears to be to show the best attitude to adopt when testing ideas.

It seems clear that to make sense of Gardner's book as whole, we need to be clear what he thinks he is saying — that is, to try grasping what moral fiction might have meant to Gardner the renegade theorist-novelist. The difficulty lies in the looseness with which he defines certain terms central to his argument. Yet, because we are set on taking Gardner seriously, we should perhaps attempt to tighten and delimit the concepts he presents as crucial to the message of *On Moral Fiction*. Much of this work will appear to be highly critical of Gardner. However, the criticisms are leveled at

---

[8] John Gardner, qtd. in Silesky, *John Gardner: Literary Outlaw*, 254.

the way the message is presented, and not the message itself.

Theorizing the Good

Moral fiction strives for the Good, the True, and the Beautiful. Yet these are not things "that exist in the way llamas do, but values which exist when embodied and, furthermore, recognized as embodied" (133). Gardner defines these values metaphorically, elliptically, negatively. Let us look at the Good and the True in particular — the Beautiful is insufficiently developed in Gardner's book and he seems to take for granted that we know precisely what he means by it.

To start with the Good, it "cannot be approached except by imagination because our understanding of it arises out of our experience of an infinite number of particular situations" (140). Gardner's concern is with promoting the Good through fiction. He takes as his model the relationships between adults that we might call healthy: "Healthy relationships between adults are characterized by sympathy and trust and are supported on both sides by maturity" (136). Gardner is implying, as I read it, that healthy adult relationships need not all be the exact same — but they are structured in a certain way, and this structure's foundation is made of trust, sympathy, and other commonsensically virtuous ideas. We do not have to be aware at all times of how the structure of a relationship determines that relationship's development. All that is needed is for the structure to be in place, so that the relationship might blossom. If this is Gardner's point — that certain psychological elements must be in place as conditions for a healthy relationship — then the first thing to point out is that as an illustration this is too elaborate to be particularly enlightening. Moral fiction is fiction that puts in place (or, structures) the necessary conditions for the reader to decide, on their own, to be moral. Rather than preach, it leads by example: it shows us characters struggling to make the right choice in difficult situations; it shows us characters we should wish to emulate. It is heavily metaphorical; it stands for a multiplicity of human experiences. That is one way to begin to theorize the Good: it is normative to the extent that it presents us with ways of thinking about moral issues, ways of behaving morally — by choice. The moral content of any particular text is not as important as the very fact that the text is morally structured. We will return to the idea of a moral structure soon.

The Good "presents a goal for the human condition here in this world, a conceptual abstraction of our actual experience of moments of good in human life; it is the essential subject of all literature, even of a strict imagist poem which asserts nothing but the value of seeing, but not all literature illustrates it: badly thought out literature obscures it, and nihilistic literature perniciously denies it" (136). It is not controversial to assume, given Gardner's pronouncements on the Good, that whatever "nihilistic literature" is, it aligns itself with evil. The implicit opposition here between good and evil places the discussion in a quasi-religious frame. Perhaps "mystical" is more appropriate, since there is an element of wonderment at the power of art peppered throughout Gardner's text. More precisely, there seems to be a core that is totally inassimilable in great art, something we cannot symbolize — an aspect beyond what the critic or even the artist can claim about the artwork. This mystical kernel lurking within or behind the artwork, of course, must remain an enigma. It also makes the task of making sense of Gardner more difficult.

The Good in art appears to belong to the incommunicable realm of intuitions, inferences, transcendence. It informs the most intimately subjective level of experience — "deep experience," as Gardner calls it (162) — and also reaches far beyond it, to shape more than just my experience or yours. It pulsates, shifts, but remains essentially directed at the betterment of human life. It resonates throughout the ages wearing different masks but speaking in the same voice. "The idea of an imperishable form for the Good has always been appealing, since it keeps the Good from changing with governments and hair styles; but actually we need not invent ghosts to keep things relatively stable" (137).

The Good is stable because the predicament in which humanity finds itself does not change at a fundamental level. This is fair enough in principle, in casual conversation. It is not good enough, however, at a theoretical level. In fact it seems chimerical. It implies something removed from the human but subtly influencing it from the outside and the inside simultaneously. We can either aim for it or reject it, but its existence, to Gardner, is beyond question so long as mankind is around to grapple with it. "The Good is existential in the sense that its existence depends upon man's" (137) — without man there is no good, but without the Good man is maladjusted, misshapen. What this amounts to is a conception of the human as inseparable from humanity's values. This in itself is not a unique perspective, but something seems confused in the argument. The Good is enigmatic, elusive but always present, of man but not of man — what, then, is its use, except as an empty word Gardner uses to absorb any contradictions that might surface in his reasoning?

This is not necessarily to deny that there can be goodness. But the Good, as a concept, means everything and very little at the same time. It is compromised by its vagueness. The serious use to which Gardner puts the Good is unconvincing. Yet a different but related problem surfaces here, the problem of goodness itself — not morality as an abstract category, but the vast trove of everyday situations where a fable, a metaphor, a simple anecdote can lead people to do "the right thing," to behave in a manner we can agree is good, conducive to the betterment of their situation.

We see Gardner trying to reconcile the impulse to goodness, the will to altruism that is sometimes evident in even the most selfish person, with the seriously complicated problem of justifying any action at all on purely philosophical grounds. In lived experience we encounter good-natured human beings doing "bad" things, and cruel individuals being "good" or in some way helpful to their community.

Gardner the writer is caught in a complex situation, and *On Moral Fiction* reads like a text offered by someone whose allegiance is to practical matters, to art as a good thing according to the standards of his time and culture. There is no categorical imperative. As the many quotations I have chosen demonstrate, Gardner's view is that we are weak but beautiful, and capable of deciphering for ourselves what a situation requires. The lack of universality here, the near-total absence of fundamental moral codes, is precisely what allows for moral fiction as an art form to claim its importance. Through the carefully chosen written word — through the novel written according to its own processes, as Gardner would have it — the reader is able to learn to understand the author's intentions, the protagonist's choices, the story's outcome. Sense, or a sense of sense, an impression of meaning, is generated in moral fiction. If this is a correct reading of Gardner's position — that is, if in the end moral fiction helps and guides us in our daily lives but does not prescribe a mode of conduct — then, if nothing else, this is an intuitive and attractive idea. It appeals to the heart instead of reason, and it feels acceptable, at least to this reader. Sadly, Gardner's position is immediately jeopardized by the second important force at play in the universe of moral fiction: the True.

Theorizing the True

"The conclusive answering of a question has to do not with the Good but with the True," Gardner declares. "Whereas we intuit the Good, we approach the unattainable and thus relative absolute 'Truth' through reason" (139). To avoid being unfair to Gardner at the outset, let us point out now that he is quick to insist that "truth is not the highest concern of fiction" (141). Nevertheless, one wonders what the point of bringing "truth" into this is. Gardner brings in certain epistemological questions which, unsurprisingly, he does not answer in a satisfactory way. Although he spends little time dealing with the True, he dwells on it just long enough to make it seem like an important category. He defines truth as "that which can be known for certain, an object of reason and analysis" (140). More: "Absolute Truth is all that could be known by an omniscient mind, and insofar as the universe contains voluntary agents and a random evolution of everything from brute matter to conscious thought, Truth is relative in the same manner as is Goodness" (140). Whatever one makes of this, it seems appropriate to say that Gardner's words imply a variety of enormous presuppositions of the sort philosophers have wrestled with for many centuries, and which he promptly sweeps under the carpet. Setting aside the question of whether anything "can be known for certain" quite as simply as Gardner assumes, since that is a different debate, there is still the problem of the relativity of a truth that can be known for certain.

What, exactly, does Gardner mean to say here? Perhaps merely that if there is such a thing as absolute truth, we are left with no choice but to have it in incomplete form, since we are not "an omniscient mind" and cannot claim to know everything (let alone anything). Or perhaps Gardner wishes to say that through "reason and analysis" we might come up with our own interpretation of an absolute truth, and that this interpretation could be valid. That Gardner appears to treat absolute truth as a sort of ontological substance is problematic enough, or at least curiously old-fashioned; the matter is not helped by his reckless refusal to argue his way to any position of credibility. By the next paragraph, Gardner has moved on to the idea of mimesis and its relation to truth and to the text. But we should not follow Gardner too eagerly here, and must instead ask about the True: what has it to do with moral fiction, or even with what he calls moral criticism?

For the implication is that the True lies beyond "mere" morality and beyond even subjective experience, relative though Gardner may claim it to be. The True, "that which can be known for certain," presumably does not center only on questions of morality; surely it would encompass much more than that. Indeed the True, as Gardner has defined it so far, would appear to lurk hidden in the very energy of human action, informing not just what we can do and know, but more relevantly, what is good and what is beautiful — it should help us decipher in the silence of the universe the judgments that we ought to make in the name of truth.

These are elementary remarks, but they are not even addressed by Gardner in his brief treatment of the True. Instead, having brought into the room this enormous animal, Gardner simply takes us into the next room and resumes his sermon: successful mimesis in art, "accurate imitation of the world" (140), can be pleasurable, he writes, but it is not crucial. He then summons up a distinction that begins, if tentatively, to clarify his position on the True: "when talking about art we use the word truth in two ways: to mean that which is factually accurate or logically valid" — the True as a limit to falsehood, as the perhaps unattainable cure for misinterpretation — and also "to mean that which does not feel like lying" (142). A few sentences later, Gardner simply stops writing about the True. Nevertheless, he has let out a clue: what he is aiming for is not so much "truth" as a state of accordance with what is, but rather a feeling of genuineness, of authenticity. The True, in Gardner's naively schematic view, is more than factuality. It is, more archaically, truthfulness. A reader should have a gut impression of having touched upon something fundamental about the world when reading a work of moral fiction. The True is manifested in our intuition that, yes, that is what it's like, that what we are reading is handling its subject sensitively and honestly. Unfortunately, such a feeling is not enough to warrant bringing all of truth into the debate. At any rate, it is not enough in the sense that linking the True to a gut feeling that something "does not feel like lying" amounts to very little. One suspects that the True ought to have been left out entirely. The problem is that without reference to truth, moral fiction would seem to lose its privileged status. If part of the point of moral fiction is to show us new ways of tackling moral problems and living morally, then surely there are certain standards of morality to which fiction must strive. They may not be absolute in the way that the Ten Commandments are absolute, but nevertheless the fiction championed by Gardner needs a set of standards if it is to strive towards anything except self-relation, self-reference — that is, more than the logic that the fiction itself creates.

Yet perhaps this is the point. Perhaps the True, beyond the mere feeling that something is not a lie (a poetically interesting but in this context useless formulation) amounts, in Gardner's schema, to a structural limit rather than anything external to the text. The only way we can salvage the True as defined in *On Moral Fiction* is to qualify Gardner's claim that the True is "that which can be known for certain, an object of reason and analysis" by adding: in the universe depicted in the fiction. This is a deliberate misreading. Curiously, it is also consistent with other statements made by Gardner in his work. If we accept that moral fiction follows its own rules to the end, or that it is the kind of narrative storytelling concerned with characters in certain situations set up by the author behaving in believable and understandable ways, then the True (as a gut feeling that the story's progress is "not a lie" and as a reaching towards a kind of absoluteness in humanity's codes and beliefs) makes some sense. It makes sense precisely as an "untrue truth" or the likeness of verisimilitude made possible by the novel. The True, here, can be seen as that which, in the logic of the fictional universe, seems plausible and realistic even though the universe depicted is a construction. The True, then, makes sense as the uninterrupted flow of what Gardner repeatedly called the "fictive dream" elsewhere.

Fiction as a dream is hardly a controversial notion, but Gardner places such importance on it that it needs to be examined to see if our qualification of his use of the True holds up. In an earlier text intended as a pedagogical exposition of the "art of fiction," Gardner claims that in fiction "the writer's first job is to convince the reader that the events he recounts really happened, or to persuade the reader that they might have happened."[9] As soon as the reader accepts the terms of buying into the lie, he also consents to dreaming the events depicted as though the dream sprang from within his being. Good fiction writing, for Gardner, is writing that succeeds in maintaining the dream's hold on the reader until the end. That is good fiction; but then what is moral fiction? In a passage in *The Art of Fiction* anticipating the themes of *On Moral Fiction*, Gardner suggests, "fiction provides, at its best, trustworthy but inexpressible models. We ingest metaphors of good, wordlessly learning to behave more like Levin than Anna . . . , more like the transformed Emma . . . than the Emma we first meet in the book."[10] Crucially, he adds: "This subtle, for the most part wordless knowledge is the 'truth' great fiction seeks out."[11] The truth explored by fiction is not Truth as a general, abstract, impossibly complicated idea, but the unreal and fictionally constructed "reality" of the universe depicted in a novel. We do not know the Truth about this or that, nor can we legitimately speak about the Truth without a variety of complications, but

---

[9] John Gardner, *The Art of Fiction: Notes on Craft for Young Writers* (New York: Vintage, 1991), 22.
[10] Gardner, *The Art of Fiction*, 63.
[11] Gardner, *The Art of Fiction*, 63.

for Gardner, a well-written novel reveals to us certain structures, rules and "truths" about its characters and situations. The truth inside a novel can thus be explained as the "unwritten" set of codes that make a novel internally consistent on its own and, by extension, rewarding and stimulating and "not phony" for the reader.

If this is a correct interpretation, then yes, the True as Gardner originally presents it in *On Moral Fiction* does have a role to play. It is simply not the role that Gardner thought it was, and sadly that is Gardner's own shortcoming. We can nevertheless see that the True (as that network of secret rules and compromises dealt with by the author to ensure that his fiction seems convincing even when set in a holiday resort on another planet), even if it is not yet formalized or well enough explored, has a place in Gardner's system. In the last instance, perhaps it would have been better to call it the Truthful rather than the True.

Is Moral Fiction the Fiction of Moralists?

A short essay by Milan Kundera cautions against simple mockery of that old-fashioned (one might say: reactionary) school of criticism capable, for example, of dismissing Madame Bovary as an immoral text. Immoral, that is, because unsafe, not pregnant with uplifting messages about the potential for human redemption. Kundera, a careful craftsman whose experiences with social realism in the arts left him desirous of something more honest and less prescriptive, is well placed to judge the merits of moralism in fiction. He chooses to write on Madame Bovary because although it is a peculiarly immoral (or amoral) text if one reads it for moral consolation, it is at the same time decidedly not a work of nihilism, cynicism or, indeed, profound immorality. However, Kundera does not lampoon the reactionary literati of Flaubert's time because he knows the transformative power of a truly impressive novel. "Is it really so inappropriate for the most prestigious French critic of his time to exhort a young writer to 'uplift' and 'console' his readers by a 'picture of goodness,' readers who deserve, as do we all, a little sympathy and encouragement?"[12] No doubt Gardner would have been inclined to agree that we all deserve sympathy and encouragement as readers, as human beings; and granting sympathy and encouragement does not have to mean telling people what to do.

When George Sand chides Flaubert (unfairly, one feels) with her condescending assertion that, "Art is not only criticism and satire"[13] — when, that is, the moralist finds fault with a work like Madame Bovary because the work in question resists easy, ready-made moralistic interpretations — that is when Gardner's thought becomes truly useful. Moral fiction, we have seen, is not the fiction of preachers and soapbox hogs. It does, however, pave the way for optimism and order. Gardner may not have been at his most rigorous in his discussions of the Good, the True, and the Beautiful, but his sincerity is beyond question. Art is not only criticism and satire, but neither, at its best, is it insincere, impersonal consolation. It's easy to suspect, by the end of *On Moral Fiction*, that moral fiction of the Gardnerian variety is really little more than the kind of writing meant to open up possibilities for the affirmation of love and life. This sounds grandiose, and in a sense it is. It is also one of *On Moral Fiction*'s most

---

[12] Milan Kundera, *The Curtain: An Essay in Seven Parts*, trans. Linda Asher (London: Faber and Faber, 2007), 60.
[13] Kundera, *The Curtain*, 60.

recurrent and important themes. A look at some examples outside of Gardner's text will show that the life-affirming potential of art, of which Gardner makes a great deal, is not quite so mystical and confused a notion as the tools Gardner uses to explain it.

A simple, effective definition of "moral fiction" does not emerge from Gardner's text. It is, however, to be found in Kundera's essay on the novel. It is Kundera who comes a bit closer to showing what moral fiction is. Whereas Gardner invokes the abstractions of the Good and the True and the Beautiful, and attacks other novelists for failing to meet standards he has not clearly set, Kundera's approach is to show, historically, where "novelistic thinking" took over the writing of fiction and became its own category with its own codes. Flaubert, and after him Musil and Broch, and many others, became novelists who produced novels as art, instead of writers who happened to write novels. They discovered the importance of letting the process of "novelistic thinking" take over. Recall once again Gardner's remark that "Art, in sworn opposition to chaos, discovers by its process what it can say. That is art's morality." Compare that to Kundera's words:

> novelistic thinking . . . has nothing to do with the thinking of a scientist or a philosopher; I would even say it is purposely a-philosophic, even antiphilo-

> sophic, that is to say fiercely independent of any system of preconceived ideas; it does not judge; it does not proclaim truths; it questions, it marvels, it plumbs; its form is highly diverse: metaphoric, ironic, hypothetic, hyperbolic, aphoristic, droll, provocative, fanciful; and mainly it never leaves the magic circle of its characters' lives; those lives feed it and justify it.[14]

By now it is clear that the type of fiction we are dealing with is born of curiosity and wonderment. The most "Gardnerian" thing about Kundera's words, however, is not the attitude that is being privileged, but rather the absence of an attitude; the writer must put aside "any system of preconceived ideas" before writing his first word. The implications are many: a writer of fiction should not set out to prove something; he should not use his characters as vehicles for his own prejudices; he should not create situations only to resolve them in his mind before the writing has started; he should not, in short, have a clear idea of what he wants to say in his work, but ought instead to find out what he wants to say. The internal logic of a work of fiction should not depend on its author's omniscience. In its broadest sense, the task of moral fiction is a negative one: moral

---

[14] Kundera, *The Curtain*, 71.

fiction avoids bringing the givens of the world into its conception. A story should not, that is, seek from the outset to reaffirm the values we all take for granted.

Moral Fiction and Plot

Gerard Manley Hopkins, in a letter, gives his opinion of Robert Louis Stevenson. It is an interesting opinion because it expresses many of the same sentiments concerning good fiction that we find in Gardner and Kundera:

> His doctrine, if I apprehend him, is something like this. The essence of Romance is incident and that only, the type of pure Romance of the Arabian Nights: those stories have no moral, no character-drawing, they run altogether on interesting incident. The incidents must of course have a connection, but it need be nothing more than that they happen to the same person, are aggravations and so on. As history consists essentially of events likely or unlikely, consequences of causes chronicled before or what may be called chance, just retributions or nothing of the sort, so Romance, which is fictitious history, consists of event, of incident. His own stories are written on this principle; they are very good and he has all the gifts a writer of fiction should have, and at first you notice no more than an ordinary well told story, but on looking back in the

> light of this doctrine you see that the persons illustrate the incident or strains of incident, the plot, the story, not the story and incidents the persons.[15]

"No moral, no character-drawing" and "running altogether on interesting incident" — in other words, the type of fiction that is immediately consumable, morally neutral, the fiction Gardner might have rejected as trivial on the grounds that it seeks to do nothing but entertain. Hopkins's comments are very much of the variety frequently made by writers about fiction. Hopkins's disapproval of fiction that relies on "incident and that only" pre-empts Gardner's own criticisms of much fiction. However, it is interesting that neither Hopkins nor Gardner dismisses plot; only the kind of fiction where "the persons illustrate the incident or strains of incident."

Gardner was happy to admit that plot is essential. He never treated plot as anything other than crucial, in fact: "Though character is the emotional core of great fiction, and though action with no meaning beyond its brute existence can have no lasting appeal, plot is — or must sooner or later become — the focus of

---

[15] Gerard Manley Hopkins, *The Correspondence of Gerard Manley Hopkins and Richard Watson Dixon*, ed. Claude C. Abbot (Oxford: Oxford University Press, 1935), 114.

every good writer's plan."[16] Plot is not an enemy of moral fiction. The structure, the pace and the chronological sequence in a novel are all important, and Gardner never says anything to the contrary. But they should not be ends in themselves; they should, rather, be the means used to show a reader what a character is capable of. The plot should bring out the life of the novel, force its characters to move and speak and make decisions. Of course, a plot does not need to be extraordinarily elaborate to achieve this, nor does it have to be terribly riveting from the start. What matters is that the plot is used to give the novel a reason to move forward. "We can enjoy a story that has some secret logic we sense but cannot immediately guess; but if we begin to suspect that the basis of profluence is nothing but mad whimsey, we begin to be distracted from the fictional dream by our questions, doubts and puzzlement, our feeling that the story is getting nowhere."[17]

---

[16] Gardner, *The Art of Fiction*, 56.
[17] Gardner, *The Art of Fiction*, 168.

Writers of Fiction and Writers of Criticism

Important theorists of the novel who are also practicing novelists have, in general, tended to downplay the intellectual aspects of writing in favor of the "organic" or holistic side of creative composition. Gardner is not the only fiction writer who shared strong views on what writing is and should be, and if he is still a bit notorious today, he is not regarded as particularly influential in comparison, say, to Henry James. And yet, James was in various ways strikingly similar in his views on the purpose of fiction to Gardner. He, too, found a certain intellectualizing tendency on the part of critics to mar the effect of well-written fiction; a century before Gardner he was already insisting on the necessity of an "organic" form in the novel: "I cannot imagine composition existing in a series of blocks . . . . A novel is a living thing, all one and continuous, like any other organism, and in proportion as it lives will it be found, I think, that in each of the parts there is something of each of the other parts."[18] Like Gardner, James prioritized the act of creation, with its

---

[18] Henry James, qtd. in Peter Rawlings, *American Theorists of the Novel* (New York: Routledge, 2006), 23.

multiplicity of explorations and dead-ends, over the simple transmission of a message, which can so easily be "moralistic" and hence, in Gardner's distinction, decidedly not "moral."

"There is one point at which the moral sense and the artistic sense lie very near together," James writes. "That is in the light of the very obvious truth that the deepest quality of a work of art will always be the quality of the mind of the producer . . . . No good novel will ever proceed from a superficial mind."[19] The tone of this declaration, along with the implicit disdain for "popular" literature — all of this brings to mind *On Moral Fiction*. And if James rejects the "dull dispute over the 'immoral' subject and the moral,"[20] this needs to be understood in its context. He developed his most trenchant criticisms of the moral/immoral distinction in response to the prescriptive and influential essay by Walter Besant, "The Art of Fiction," in which Besant declared that fiction ought to have "a conscious moral purpose"[21] —

---

[19] James, qtd. in Rawlings, *American Theorists of the Novel*, 25.

[20] Henry James, "Preface to 'The Portrait of a Lady,'" in *The Art of the Novel: Critical Prefaces by Henry James* (Chicago: University of Chicago Press, 2011), 45.

[21] Walter Besant, qtd. in John Goode, "Walter Besant and Henry James," in *Tradition and Tolerance in Nineteenth Century Fiction*, eds. David Howard, John

ambiguous wording, but given that Besant insists on proper art being "governed and directed by general laws"[22] we can be sure he is not in agreement with James and Gardner on the need for an "organic" development of a novel. That there are no clearly delineated solutions for moral problems to be found in fiction is a recurring argument made by many important fiction writers; James is just one of the most outspoken of these.

This line of thinking recalls Gardner's (and Kundera's) emphasis on the probing nature of fiction. As we have seen, what Gardner calls "moral fiction" is at its barest simply the kind of fiction that opens up moral questions without attempting to answer them from the start. It probes; it follows the rules it set out for itself instead of following the normative, common sense moral commandments of the society from which it emerged. Though this is a loose and not extraordinarily useful definition, it points to an attitude common to many novelists and strangely lacking in many critics who are not practitioners of fiction; the attitude of "knowing that you don't know" and being content to discover what you have to say through your writing, instead of writing because you already know what you wish to say.

Lucas, and John Goode (New York: Routledge, 1966), 255 [243–81].

[22] Besant, qtd. in Goode, "Walter Besant and Henry James," 256.

It is a decidedly unacademic way of doing things, and that must surely be one of the reasons texts like *On Moral Fiction* prove inspiring to novelists but not to critics. David Guterson, Raymond Carver, Lore Segal, John L'Heureux and many other novelists have paid tribute to Gardner (a quick glance at the blurbs on copies of Gardner's didactic books makes this clear), but few professional literary critics have done the same.

Perhaps Albert Camus was playing the role of the "serious novelist" when he said in an interview, "I don't claim to teach anybody! Whoever thinks this is mistaken. The problems confronting young people today are the same ones confronting me, that is all. And I am far from having solved them."[23] This kind of modesty may well seem a tad disingenuous to a critic like John Krapp, who argues that, "Camus cannot sincerely evade complicity in the morally instructive dimension of his work,"[24] but Camus is only joining the chorus of fiction writers whose interest is in asking questions, not forcing answers. This is not a difficult concept to understand, but it seems deeply problematic for critics in that it both oversimplifies the many processes going on in a "literary text" (James's novels are not as "easy

---

[23] Albert Camus, qtd. in John Krapp, *An Aesthetics of Morality* (Columbia: University of South Carolina Press, 2002), 76.
[24] Camus, qtd. in Krapp, *An Aesthetics of Morality*, 76.

to read" as one might assume from his comments on the need for an intuitive, organic flow in fiction) and it confuses the task of fiction in general by submitting it to a loose set of criteria based on whether it preaches or just suggests. In the end, when a novelist like Gardner sets out, paradoxically, to preach about the need for fiction that does not preach (but which still has a moral intent), he is laying bare a problem that seems insoluble. He is tackling, in a slightly naïve and overbearing way, the issue of what art should be doing to its audience — an issue that very few people agree on. That is why the false modesty of Camus's comments can still seem convincing, or why the vague and untheorizable, unprescriptive essays on the craft by Henry James and others are never completely satisfying. Gardner may have gone about things in a heavy-handed and even boorish manner when he released *On Moral Fiction*, but the controversy it provoked reveals a deep unease in literary criticism with the incompatibility between what an author sets out to do and what a text becomes in the hands of the critic.

It is an enormous topic, and in the end it is of course not the only reason *On Moral Fiction* has been relegated to the dustbins. Gardner raised big issues, and although he dared to tackle them in his book, he did not succeed in convincing his critics that he was anything more than an apologist for a certain literary conservatism. Even Wayne C Booth, whose work on the "ethics of fiction" sometimes shares a great deal with Gardner's thought even if he seems to downplay this, limited his commentary on Gardner to pithy remarks: "It is clear that the only acceptable fiction will be whatever meets his announced moral standards. He always implies that one might arrive at his secure judgments by the same logic with which he defends them, as if working out a simple implied syllogism."[25] This is not a fair assessment of *On Moral Fiction*; it ignores the very heart of Gardner's message — that there is no clear-cut, logical way to arrive at moral judgments in literature. These judgments must be arrived at, quite tentatively, through a process that involves writer and reader, character and plot, particular and universal. If it were a matter of syllogistic deduction, the very process of fiction would be a non-art, a scientific method.

Gardner's argument, which is unquestionably confused in places, is still not so stern and uncompromising that Gardner ought to be lumped in with Plato and other "overtly ethical critics" who, "having experienced some offering that feels unquestionably threatening or harmful to the spirit," try "to damn it as the

---

[25] Wayne C. Booth, *The Company We Keep* (Berkeley: University of California Press, 1988), 54.

unfailing source of artistic evil."[26] This is caricature. There is little that can legitimately be considered normative in what Gardner is saying. Yet if there is such a limited understanding of what he is saying, then the fault must lie with Gardner as well. *On Moral Fiction* would, I think, have benefited from some prolonged and serious analyses of at least three or four works of fiction; furthermore, it might have been wiser on Gardner's part to avoid such a polemical tone. As Foucault puts it, the polemicist

> proceeds encased in privileges that he possesses in advance and will never agree to question. On principle, he possesses rights authorizing him to wage war and making that struggle a just undertaking; the person he confronts is not a partner in the search for truth, but an adversary, an enemy who is wrong, who is harmful and whose very existence constitutes a threat.[27]

Gardner fits this description in some of *On Moral Fiction*'s less nuanced passages, and if we choose to ignore this problem, we do so in the

---

[26] Booth, *The Company We Keep*, 51.
[27] Michel Foucault, "Polemics, Problems and Problematizations: An Interview," in *The Foucault Reader*, ed. Paul Rabinow (London: Penguin, 1991), 382.

knowledge that Gardner, who championed taking the greatest care when structuring a book, and who insisted on the need to respect one's characters at least during the act of writing, often failed to take his own advice in the moment of giving the advice. He, too, caricatured all the William Gasses and the John Barthes with whom he took issue. He, too, sometimes reduced his literary adversaries to stick figures and straw men. *On Moral Fiction*, according to the definition set forth in it, is not written very morally.

Goodnight, Gardner

Toward the very end of his life, Gardner tried to water down the passion with which he'd written *On Moral Fiction*, as if embarrassed by his earlier enthusiasm. He eventually summed up his entire position very simply:

> Every time a really good movie comes along . . . everybody starts imitating the hero. . . . If the hero or the central character in a novel is a whiner who can't get out of bed, who sees nothing but evil in the world, who thinks everybody is a hypocrite, and so on, the people who imitate him are going to destroy themselves because they are wrong about reality. I think that presenting sort of noble models of behavior, which is not to say perfect people . . . you give people a model for their own lives, for their own feelings.[28]

The pity of this is that although Gardner can sound like a "whiner" himself, someone "who thinks everybody is a hypocrite," the most salient parts of *On Moral Fiction* are not only

---

[28] Gardner, "Interview with the English Department of Pan American University," 260.

inspiring and encouraging, but also deserving of a wider audience, an audience that Gardner's didactic books, like *On Becoming a Novelist*, still occasionally find. Gardner, in *On Moral Fiction*, works against himself, and his enthusiasm and optimism get ignored along the way. The book, once so controversial, is now as good as out of print, and many of the authors Gardner picked on when he was writing it (Katherine Anne Porter, Robert Coover, even John Updike and William Gaddis) seem to have faded from critical attention significantly. Perhaps this should teach us how crucial it is to be humble, the way Gardner was not. More generously, we could say that Gardner misunderstood his audience and his audience misunderstood him. There must be some truth to this — the example of Wayne C. Booth would demonstrate it. But the ultimate test of Gardner's vision is the lasting appeal of the novels written as if according to his standards. These are bizarre and powerful and memorable in their own right, and Gardner's greatest contribution might very well be his idiosyncratic understanding of what makes them so strong.

But perhaps the sincerest thing that I can do for Gardner here is to acknowledge his influence on me. That is what he would have wanted, anyway: for people to "get it" even if he hadn't articulated things particularly well. *On Moral Fiction*, so far as it is remembered from time to time, will remain a troubling book for many people — but once in a while he will appeal to a young novelist in a profound way, far more profoundly than those who ridicule Gardner might suspect. It remains a wordless thing, of course. Take away the Good, the True, the Beautiful and all of that pseudo-theorizing and you are left with an experienced, flawed novelist asking people to remember to like life, and to like people. It isn't fashionable, but it'll do.

REFERENCES

Booth, Wayne C. 1988. *The Company We Keep*. Berkeley: University of California Press.

Foucault, Michel. 1991. "Polemics, Problems and Problematizations: An Interview." In *The Foucault Reader*, ed. Paul Rabinow. London: Penguin.

Gardner, John. [1978] 2000. *On Moral Fiction*. New York: Basic Books.

Gardner, John. 1990. "Interview with John Gardner, English Department of Pan American University (1981)." In *Conversations with John Gardner*, ed. Allan Chavkin. Jackson: University Press of Mississippi.

Gardner, John. 1991. *The Art of Fiction: Notes on Craft for Young Writers*. New York: Vintage.

Goode, John. 1966. "Walter Besant and Henry James." In *Tradition and Tolerance in*

Nineteenth Century Fiction, eds. David Howard, John Lucas, and John Goode. New York: Routledge. 243–81.

Hegel, Georg W. F. 1977. *The Phenomenology of Spirit*, trans. Arthur V. Miller. Oxford: Oxford University Press, 1977.

Hopkins, Gerard Manley. 1935. *The Correspondence of Gerard Manley Hopkins and Richard Watson Dixon*, ed. Claude C. Abbot. Oxford: Oxford University Press.

James, Henry. 2011. *The Art of the Novel: Critical Prefaces by Henry James*. Chicago: University of Chicago Press.

Krapp, John. 2002. *An Aesthetics of Morality*. Columbia: University of South Carolina Press.

Kundera, Milan. 2007. *The Curtain: An Essay in Seven Parts*, trans. Linda Asher. London: Faber and Faber.

Rawlings, Peter. 2006. *American Theorists of the Novel*. New York: Routledge.

Silesky, Barry. 2004. *John Gardner: Literary Outlaw*. Chapel Hill: Algonquin.

W. dreams, like Phaedrus, of an army of thinker-friends, thinker-lovers. He dreams of a thought-army, a thought-pack, which would storm the philosophical Houses of Parliament. He dreams of Tartars from the philosophical steppes, of thought-barbarians, thought-outsiders. What distances would shine in their eyes!

~Lars Iyer

www.babelworkinggroup.org

Watch with both eyes . . .

. . cows and wars and chewing gum and mountains

www.ingramcontent.com/pod-product-compliance
Lightning Source LLC
Chambersburg PA
CBHW070850160426
43192CB00012B/2379